IMAGES OF
CHORLEY

IMAGES OF
CHORLEY

**The
Chorley Guardian
Co. Ltd.**

Associate Editor
George Birtill

Breedon Books
Publishing Company
Limited

First published in Great Britain by
The Breedon Books Publishing Company Limited
44 Friar Gate, Derby, DE1 1DA.
1994

ISBN 1 873626 82 7

Printed and bound by Butler & Tanner, Frome and London.
Cover printed by BDC Printing Services Limited of Derby

Contents

Foreword

I T IS not often that Chorley gets a chance to boast about its proud past. So it is a privilege to be able to offer this pictorial record of the town and its people.

We hope that, as readers turn the pages, the faces which feature in the photographs will unlock memories of their childhood and families. And we hope that scenes of yesteryear, of buildings and streets, of events and everyday life, will stir half-forgotten folk tales.

The various sections of the book try to capture the many faces of Chorley's rich past: the town at work, at play, in celebration and sadness.

This book has been put together with affection for the town of Chorley in order that it can be enjoyed by the people of Chorley and surrounding villages.

Special thanks must be paid to the book's associate editor, George Birtill, for opening the files he has gathered over the years, and *Chorley Guardian* photographer Ian Robinson, whose hard work and dedication tracked down many long-forgotten photographs.

We would also like to thank, for their help and kindness, Chorley Borough Council for permission to use the files at Astley Hall; the Royal Ordnance Factory at Euxton, for opening the pictorial records of the factory at war; the Astley Hall Collection and, not least, the readers of the *Chorley Guardian*.

Steve McLean
Editor
The Chorley Guardian
September 1994

Introduction

BENEATH the towering slopes of the West Pennine Moors lies a town with a remarkable history – Chorley.

For what began as a line on the earliest and crudest of ancient maps is now a thriving and pleasant town, in the middle of some of Britain's most sophisticated communication systems and nestling among some of Lancashire's most beautiful countryside.

But Chorley – its name means 'the peasant's field' – grew from literally nothing. It was originally known as Main Brook, an area which was a territorial boundary with just a Roman road running through it from north to south. Today, that ancient route is the A6.

The first recorded borough of Chorley was created by William de Ferrers, Lord of Chorley, in 1250. By 1287, it was bigger than neighbouring Bolton but in 1332 the borough was entirely wiped out by invading Scots.

But it rose again and was handed down through three generations of the de Ferrers family to William Ferrers of Groby. He was to lose his title of Lord of the Manor and several other families were to rule until the Ferrers of Groby regained their rightful inheritance towards the end of the century. The Ferrers were to remain in power for another 100 years.

In 1641, one of the great foundations of Chorley was laid through the founding of the Chorley Grammar School but, 47 years later, the borough became enmeshed in revolution.

Parliamentary forces stormed the town and met no resistance. Richard Chorley and his son Charles, heads of the Saxon family which took its name from the town in which they lived, were arrested as supporters of James II. Richard Chorley was executed at Preston, Charles was to die in jail.

Today, Chorley is famed as a market town and it has held the right to hold markets since the 15th century. But it was also known as a town of justice, holding a court from the reign of Henry VIII through to the 18th century. Chorley's first police force was formed in 1794 when three special constables were taken on to assist the two annually-elected officers.

Chorley's growth has mainly been in the last 200 years. The first signs of industry appeared in 1769 with the expansion of the town's by now traditional hand-loom weaving.

The town became a recognised coaching centre in 1824 as growth developed, and in 1875 the new Town Hall was built. Chorley finally became recognised as a town proper in 1881. Today, the mills are silent and the mines in the surrounding villages have disappeared.

This book looks at the Chorley of yesteryear and, we hope, will inform, entertain and, in some cases, bring back happy memories of this sturdy Lancashire town.

The Streets of Chorley

The Red Lion was an old coaching house at the corner of Mealhouse Lane. Next to it is Stone's Grocery shop. Mr Stone was a prominent member of the Council. The White Hart, which replaced the Red Lion, was set back, facing Mealhouse Lane and the other buildings besides the Red Lion had to be cleared to make room.

Close to Lyon's Lane railway bridge, this row of property was known as 'Shitpot Row'. The archway down the side street led to a common backyard – the row had obviously been built, when 'petties' or loos were shared in everybody's backyard.

The building of the Chorley North Industrial Estate in the 1970s.

Bagganley Hall in 1966 – it was demolished to make way for the M61.

Steeley Lane. The Railway Hotel, on the right of the picture, featured bowling tournaments, despite the fact that the green was said to have been built over a mineshaft. In fact, before the railway was built, Clifford Street, used by the coal trucks, was called Coal Pit Lane.

The Woodlands Hostel, Southport Road. During World War Two it housed workers and afterwards accommodated foreign workers from various countries. When the new police station was built, the administrative offices were housed in the office buildings. A college now occupies part of the site.

Hunters and horses find a popular calling place at the Black Horse at Limbrick, Chorley. Two members of the Holcombe Hunt await the rest of the hunt before chasing their quarry.

An extension of the Red Lion was the Red Lion tap. It was favoured by the younger generation. Professional men preferred the 'Big House' as the Red Lion was called.

Chorley's first bonfire night since the end of World War Two was held in November 1955. Explosives and other materials used in fireworks had been restricted until then.

The former boating pond in Astley Park. In 1994, a plan to site a sewage pumping station there caused outcry. It was later defeated.

Devonshire Road was numbered from the Pall Mall End because it was mainly a footpath through fields before the St Thomas's Road end was opened in 1920. It was asphalted so that traffic noise would not interfere with St Mary's School and Church, pictured right. Since this photograph was taken, the school has moved to Walgarth Drive and Summer's corn mill, the tall building on the right, was demolished and the site used for offices.

Lyon's Lane in 1958. The mill on the right was one of the earliest in Chorley.

Some people may not recognise this. It was Lyon's Lane. The pub on the right was the Green Man Still.

In 1932 a poll was held on the Sunday opening of cinemas in Chorley. It was successful, but did not save the cinemas. Television saw to that in the 1950s and 1960s.

Temporary traffic lights were installed at the Duke Street and Lyon's Lane crossing. They were dispensed with only when the by-pass came through in 1994.

Standish Street, once known as the Irish Quarter, is now given up to the motor trade and other industries. The Hare and Hounds sign over the entrance of the building on the right is a reminder of other times.

This building served as Chorley Borough Library for more than 80 years. Demands increased to such an extent that it was agreed the County Library Service should take over. The former Chorley Grammar School and later Chorley College, proved the ideal building and the County Library Service assumed control on 12 June 1986. The old library was demolished and a health centre built on the site.

Botany Brow used to begin at these cottages (of the handloom weaver's design). They have now been demolished.

Preston Street, Chorley, was very much a community related to North Street Mills, which are no more. Everybody knew, or was related to, everybody else and as soon as the photographer erected his tripod, people came from nowhere.

The barn at Botany was near the cottages. It deals with motor repairs, but it was originally the Tithe Barn for Chorley Parish Church.

The widening of Botany Bridge over the Canal was taking place in 1934. Leonard Fairclough was the contractor, and the steam crane aroused a lot of interest.

View along Birkacre Brow taken from the entrance to the Bleachworks. Riversdale House on the left is where the mill engineer lived. Birkacre Cottage, now demolished, and Sunnymount are on the right. On the left is the wall of 'The Cottage' garden. The mill manager, Mr Stafford, lived there. This picture was taken in 1934.

Group of children photographed on the Preston Road, Whittle.

View looking down Birkacre Brow. Riversdale is on the right, Birkacre Cottages, now demolished, on the left. In the foreground a soldier is pushing a bicycle. Further down is a side-car with a wicker chair . The picture was taken during World War One.

Going to Market

A cattle market before the turn of the century. Chorley has been a market town since the 12th century, but the cattle auctions have now gone.

By the 1960s there is little evidence of cattle sales here. During the war, the only sales were from garage stalls provided by the auctioneer. On this picture the site is occupied by the gas showroom which has now closed. The tea room on the left began when the Royal Ordnance factory was built – Irish labourers liked food when they had a drink or two.

Crowds pack Market Place at the turn of the century. Note the cart loads of goods parked between the shops and stalls.

This picture of the covered stalls is taken from the opposite direction, swinging towards Fazakerley Street and the Town Hall.

Decimalisation arrives in Chorley. From 1971, all market prices were shown in old pence and new currency.

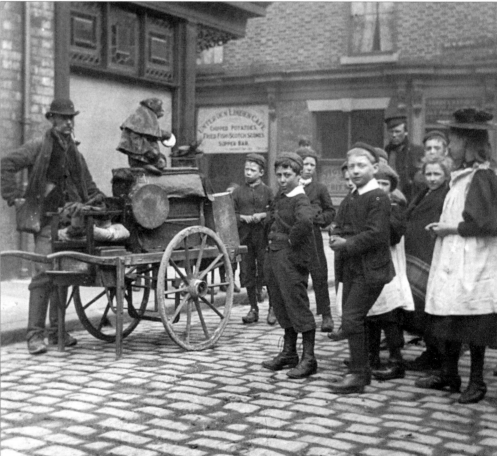

Children gather before one of the most popular attractions – an organ grinder and live monkey. The Linden café in the background advertised its chipped potatoes, fried fish, Scotch scones and suppers.

13 September 1957 – this big wheel provided a miniature Chorley illuminations, and was erected on the cattle market where another big wheel had been previously sited.

Down Market Street

The Odeon Cinema, Market Street, in 1955. A poll was conducted on whether films should be allowed to be shown on Sundays.

A postcard of Chapel Street, Chorley. The date stamp is 1908. St Mary's Church towers in the background.

The Prince Albert in Market
Street, between Halliwell Street
and Anderton Street, in 1870.
The landlord in the doorway is
Thomas Gillett. He had ten sons
who formed a band to entertain
the clientele.

Chorley's famous Big
Lamp was sited at the
top of Market Street at
the junction with Pall
Mall and Bolton Road.
The much-loved lamp
was a popular meeting
place. It was taken down
and its whereabouts is
still the subject of
controversy.

A close-up view of the Big Lamp.

A view of the then cobbled Market Street, believed to be around the turn of the century. Note the horse-drawn coal cart in the left foreground.

Before the turn of the century, Chorley had its own version of Woolworth's at the corner of Fazakerley Street and Market Street. The Lyon's shop used the more famous store's policy of selling nothing for more than sixpence.

Market Street in the late 1950s. The Bulge, as it was known, on the right of the street, later disappeared as Market Street was widened.

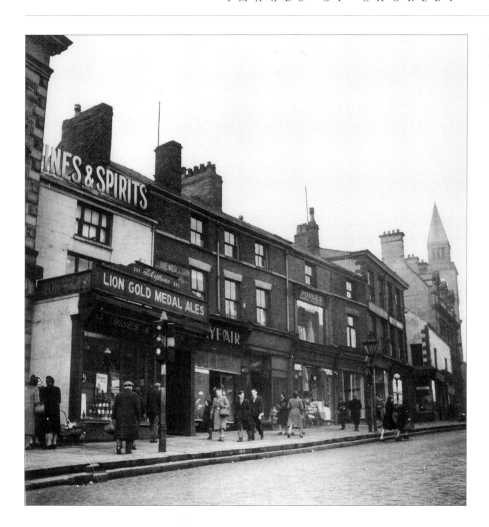

The double kerb at the top end of Market Street in the 1950s shows how high the pavement has been raised.

Market Street, pictured around the 1920s.

Mayoral procession for Bertram H.Gaskell in June 1954. He is accompanied by the Vicar of St George's, Canon Bramley, Town Clerk George Jackson and other members of the Borough Council wearing robes and caps. The Theatre Royal, later converted into a cinema, stands out down the street.

Market Street Bulge: Christie's snack bar, on the right, started what was known as the Bulge. Four shops in the row extended outwards from the line of the remaining shops. The buildings, which were declared unsafe, were demolished to widen the road.

Union Street was the busiest two-way street in the town centre. It links Market Street with the new town centre by-pass and the traffic is so heavy at times that there have been calls to re-site the Bus Station elsewhere. This picture was taken in the late 1960s.

The new bus route worked, but Chapel Street, once one-way up, became one-way down. It is now pedestrianised.

New Market Street has always been important to shoppers. Seen here as it was in the 1970s, all the buildings on the right have been demolished as part of the town centre redevelopment which began in 1994.

New Market Street had its traffic problems even when the Victoria Hotel was on the corner with Chapel Street.

Fazakerley Street was once a popular extension of Market Street. Above Hilton's shoe shop was the Kingston Café, popular with American GIs during World War Two.

Crowds used every vantage point possible to watch passing parades, including the old offices of the *Chorley Guardian* and Leons Tailors in Market Street.

Chapel Street, always the popular shopping street in Chorley. Various buildings were demolished, like the arcade on the left. Further on, Haydock's timber yards and sawmill are very obvious. This picture was taken from St Mary's tower in September 1955.

Not only was traffic hindered by a narrow Market Street but ancient buildings set too far forward obscured the ancient parish church, as this picture of the entrance to Union Street and Church Brow clearly shows.

The old Royal Oak Hotel, Market Street, was an institutional part of the town. An old coaching house, it recalled past grandeur. Chorley folk were angry at the proposal to demolish it in 1936, but apart from other considerations, the road was too narrow and the Government was calling for implementation of the town centre improvement scheme.

Steeley Lane in
the 1960s.

An old lady shopping on a
Saturday morning in 1920,
although her dress is Victorian.

The circus comes to town in May 1954 with elephants on parade in Market Street.

The junction of St Thomas's Road and Dole Lane – the buildings are now gone.

Royal Theatre, Market Street, later became a supermarket and is now a hamburger restaurant.

Cheapside in 1972. The betting shop on the right remains, although it is now owned by Stanley Racing.

Another circus arrives in town, possibly just after the turn of the century. It is believed that the legendary Buffalo Bill – former Wild West Indian fighter William Cody – may have been the star attraction at this circus, seen arriving on Market Street.

Getting Around

An Austin rally at the covered market in Market Place in 1957.

White Bear Station at Adlington, now demolished, was on the Wigan-Blackburn line which also went through Chorley. Adlington, a major population centre, is still served by its own railway station on the Preston line.

Joe Green, who worked for many years as a guardsman on the 'Chorley Bob', a train which ran from Chorley to Wigan on the old line. The picture was taken at the Stump Lane Bridge around the turn of the century.

June 1959. Chorley takes an early holiday from the old station. A train also waits at the Blackburn platform, which was later dispensed with.

The old Chorley Station and crossing in 1970. Although the signal boxman was supposed to let traffic through the level crossing, the busy line was not always safe for this. Drivers tended to save time by taking an alternative route.

A local photographer claimed to have waited ten years to get this shot of a large van crossing the line at the old Chorley Station. The crossing was the responsibility of the signalman and the line is not only busy, the approach has a sweeping curve. Most drivers found it quicker to use Lyon's Lane Bridge or some other alternative. There is no record of the gates opening since the by-pass came into use.

Complaints about Chorley Railway Station were not confined to the crossing. The whole station looked untidy and shabby, particularly the 'Elephant Tanks' used for filling boilers on steam engines.

However, the railway people took notice but removal of the platform canopy on a very draughty station was not appreciated. The picture shows the crossing gates closed to rail traffic, no consolation either.

Railway Station showing entrance to Goods Depot – 26 March 1963. The buildings have now disappeared.

Chorley Goods Depot, also now gone.

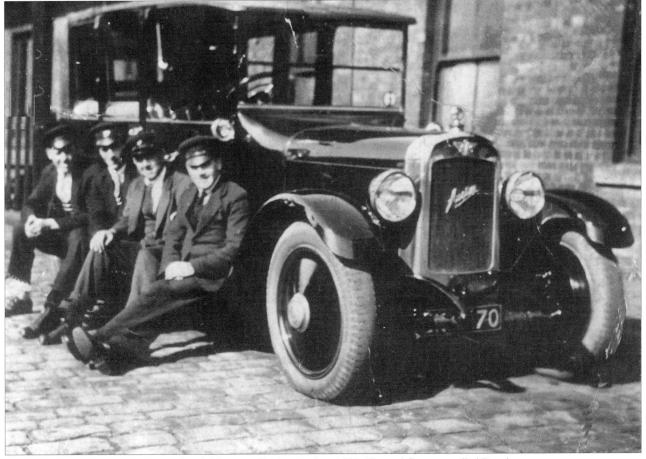

'Four Skamps' taxi drivers at Chorley Station, 1920. The taxi firm was called Bannisters.

Chorley Station, again showing the crossing gates. The date of the picture is unknown

Everybody walked to celebrate the completion of the M61, Chorley's own motorway. In October 1969, to mark its opening, crowds were allowed to walk along its length.

The M61 motorway walk, 30 October 1969.

Only seven of the nine railway arches landmark are visible from this point in Heapey Road. They carried the Chorley to Blackburn
line until it closed. The Nine Arches were demolished to make way for the M61 motorway.

Another view of the Nine Arches landmark.

When the M61 motorway was built, a larger bridge was required at Botany. The bridge was built by Fairclough's and later became
nationally known.

A group outing in a wagonette – a familiar sight in Chorley around the turn of the century. The identity of the passengers and date of the picture are unknown.

Neighbours from Geoffrey Street, Chorley, going out for a day trip in a motorised wagonette in the 1920s. They usually went to visit the countryside. The wagonette was capable of 12mph, as marked on its side.

Parsons' charabanc outside the Wheatsheaf in Coppull, 1914, taking a party on an outing.

Parsons' bus outside Yates's Wine Lodge. Mr Parsons started at Leyland Motors in Chorley, then began his own bus and charabanc service. Charabancs appeared to wait in West Street in the front of Yates's, as in this picture. The charabanc was a Vulcan model.

This petrol-driven bus belonged to the Lancashire and Yorkshire Railway Company and was a link between Chorley, Whittle-le-Woods and Bamber Bridge.

There was a steam bus service in Chorley, built by the Lancashire Steam Motor Company, Leyland, precursors of Leyland Motors Ltd.

Buses on the 'Flat Iron'. Before the first Bus Station was built in 1927, buses collected on the side near the Cattle Market.

Using the Town Hall Square as a Bus Station was not satisfactory so far as the Borough Council were concerned. In the interests of safety, Ribble were ordered to take a site near the Post Office.

The Borough allowed Ribble to lease land near the 'Flat Iron' for their first Bus Station, shown in the picture. The present Bus Station has an enlarged site.

Before the motor car dominated society, people used to queue around the Post Office for the Bus Station, particularly at holiday times. What cars there were, as in this picture taken in 1946, parked in the street. The Royal Oak car park in the foreground remained nearly empty. The Post Office has changed a bit too. The main entrance then was in High Street.

The Dallas family firm ran buses through Wheelton village until they were bought by Ribble, The bus ran every half hour to the Conservative Club at Withnell and twice on Saturdays. Mr Les Smith (right) opened the Clock Garage in 1946.

Les Smith and his taxi – an Austin 12 – taken near Dan Marsden's butcher's shop at Wheelton in 1946, the year Mr Smith opened the Clock Garage.

Staff at the famous Butty Bar – the Bus Station café – setting out on a day trip about 30 years ago. The Butty Bar, another well-known Chorley institution, was closed down in July 1994 to make way for the town centre redevelopments.

Interior of the Butty Bar at Chorley Bus Station.

Funeral carriages outside Greatorex Livery Stables before petrol was the motive power.

The Town Hall

The Chorley Town Hall Christmas Tree in 1955.

A fashion parade at the Town Hall in 1958.

An aerial set up to
provide a TV broadcast
from Chorley Town Hall.

Chorley
Town Hall
pictured in
1946.

The Assembly Room in
the Town Hall had quite a
large balcony at the rear.
Critics of the council said
it had been put there
because of acoustics. The
arrival of microphones and
amplifiers made it
superfluous and the room
was then big enough
without the balcony, so it
was removed.

St Thomas's Square in the 1960s. It became smaller when the Police HQ and Magistrates' Court were built.

The Town Hall Assembly Room complete with balcony, with all arrangements made for Chorley Boys' Club boxing tournament. The balcony is now long gone.

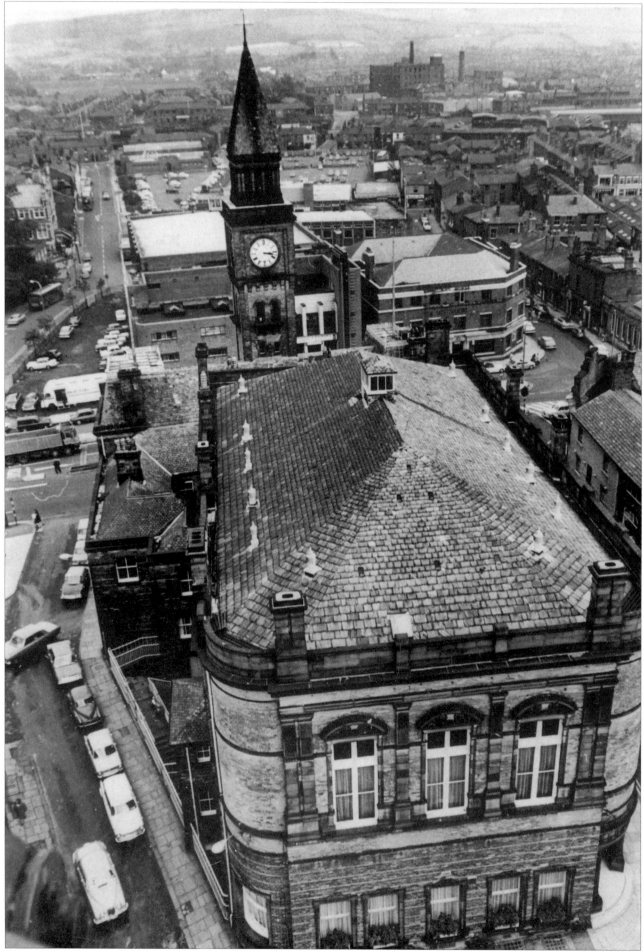

An aerial view of Chorley Town Hall.

The old Chorley Town Hall jutting out on the right, Craven's grocers (once the Police Station) and the Royal Oak, pictured in 1936.

The local fire-brigade adjust the hands of the clock on Chorley Town Hall.

Chorley Town Hall, seen from Park Road,
early 1900s.

Alderman John Green (left) pictured in
1946 studying plans for the Royal
Agricultural Show. He is with Borough
Engineer Mr W.Lowe in the Mayor's
Parlour.

Alderman John Green with Mr W.Lowe, the Borough Engineer, viewing the site for the Royal Agricultural Show at Astley Park in 1946.

The February 1946 Council Meeting
in the Council Chamber.
Left to right: Alderman Ralph Gent,
Alderman John Green (Mayor), Mr
George Jackson (Town Clerk), Mr
Roy Stringfellow (Deputy Town
Clerk).

A public meeting outside the
Town Hall, possibly in the 1940s.

Local Services

Christmas in the Rawcliffe Ward at the New Chorley Hospital, 1935. Many mill owners gave money for the hospital and much was raised through charity events and donations. There was a 'Hospital Fund' for 1d a week, which entitled the member to free treatment.

Rawcliffe Hospital, Chorley, now the Borough Council offices in Gillibrand Street.

The official opening of Chorley and District Hospital in September 1933, 40 years after the opening of the first Chorley Hospital. The opening ceremony was performed by the Earl of Crawford and Balcarres. The hospital had three wards – the Rawcliffe Ward for men, Winstanley Ward for women and the Samuel Ward for children. There was one operating theatre. Another one was added later.

In 1933, Chorley's Mayor, Mrs B.M.Gillett, launched a women's fund-raising scheme in aid of the women's ward at Chorley's new hospital. The Queen, now the Queen Mother, sent along two china jardinieres to be auctioned in aid of the fund after Buckingham Palace received a letter from Mrs Annie Gorst of Parkside Avenue, asking for help. Pictured at the handing over are Mrs Gould, left, and Mrs Gillett.

Above left: March 1963. Police dogs were a deterrent, especially during periods of trouble between youths from Chorley and neighbouring towns. Pictured are two of Chorley's best-known dogs, Anna, left, and Gary, with a handler. Right: Chorley was one of the places chosen to test the use of radio by the police. PC J.Woods was the officer who reported.

4 September 1964. The smart new uniform for women police officers did not go unnoticed!

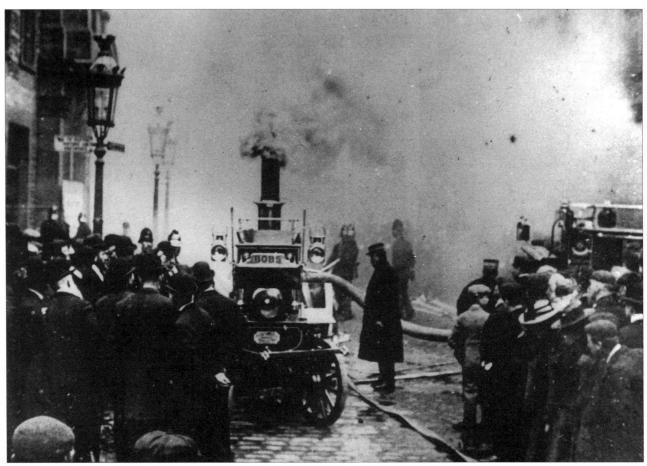

One of the first jobs tackled by the first Borough Council was to provide a fire-engine with a steam-powered pump. On 19 June 1884, everyone turned out in their in Sunday best when it was christened 'Bobs' after Lord Roberts. But getting up steam proved a dirty business and the onlookers were covered with soot and dirt.

The original Chorley Fire Station next to St George's School on Bolton Road.

An honour for John Sharples, chairman of the fire brigade committee. Mr Sharples, nearest the engine, had it named after him.

Proud and shining – a Chorley fire-engine crew in ceremonial uniform. The motorised engine was made by Leyland Motors.

Chorley people were fond of the combined Police Station and Courthouse in St Thomas's Square, but it was not nearly big enough for work that increased greatly after World War Two.

Inside Chorley Magistrates Court, St Thomas's Square, when it was sited above the Police Station. Note the spiked railings around the dock.

Industrial Chorley

The last shift on, 31 March 1967, at Chisnall Hall Colliery near Coppull. This ended coal mining in an area which had been rich in 'black diamonds'.

The last shift at the closure of Ellerbeck Colliery near Coppull, in August 1965. The last man coming out of the cage was a Mr Richardson.

Working on the looms at Jacquard Weavers in 1957.

Checking the looms at the Talbot Cotton Mill, Chorley, in the 1950s.

Rebuilt after a fire, this massive factory was still known as Heapey Bleachworks when serving a different purpose. In the end it was Whitters. The site has now been cleared for housing.

Whitters products being taken to the goods yard by horse.

Birtwistle's Mill, Abbey Village, spinning room in 1910. The lady on the right is Annie Nightingale.

Birtwistle's Mill, Abbey Village.
Eight ladies pictured in the
weaving shed in 1910.

Clara Fairhurst at work,
weaving in Rice's Mill in
1920.

Two shire horses from Birkacre won prizes at the Preston Royal Show in the 1920s. Mr Caunce, on the right, prepared the horses, and his helper John Yates is on the left.

Vincent Rogerson standing with one of the prize-winning Birkacre horses in 1922.

A group of bleaching girls sitting on a hill at Birkacre. Some of the girls, especially on the front row, look no more than ten years old.

A group of tambouring girls at Birkacre. In the middle at the back is Mrs Sarah Morris, who trained the tambourers – workers who embroidered cotton products.

The woman second from the left of this group is tambouring – embroidering a piece of cotton.

Group of bleaching girls and boys who worked in the croft, possibly in Birkacre, near Coppull, in the making-up room. The picture is from the 1920s.

Six men outside a refreshment hut, taken on Moor Road, Chorley. They may have been either miners, because of the tough clogs and watches, or mill workers.

A steam waggon taking pitmen home from Birkacre Colliery. The speed was limited to 12mph, or 5mph with a trailer attached. Date unknown.

Coming off shift at Welch Whittle Colliery in January 1960.

Farewell – miners gather to bid happy retirement to Sam Briers, centre left, on his last day at Ellerbeck Colliery in 1961.

The Royal Ordnance Factory at Euxton was built in the 1930s. This picture shows what was then described as 'the world's biggest concrete mixer' at the site in October 1937.

Filling anti-tank MkII mines during World
War Two at the ROF.

Hand stemming
500lb GP bomb at
the ROF during
World War Two.

Filling 500lb SAP bomb during World War Two.

Empty shell stores at the ROF during World War Two.

Finishing the six-inch howitzer shells at the ROF in wartime.

Filling 4.5in howitzer shells at the ROF.

Workers at the ROF fill one of the biggest devices produced at the plant – a 4,000lb bomb. But safety measurers were basic – overalls and face masks.

Chorley Churches

Croston lost its cross in Reformation times. The village blacksmith, whose workshop was nearby, had the idea of converting an old millstone into the shape of a cross which was erected on the steps already there. This was duly dedicated in September 1953.

The Men's Guild of St Mary's RC at the church club swimming pool in 1906. The enterprising Guild members volunteered to dig the 51ft x 21ft pool for free. Each paid five shillings (25p) to inscribe their name on a brick. The water in the pool, which was heated, was changed each week. It was built as an alternative to club life and the Revd T.S.Clark gave up his vinery for a changing room. The pool closed in 1938 following the opening of a Corporation-owned baths.

Bowlers at the Old St Mary's RC Church Club.

A lone cyclist pedals away from St George's Church around 1910.

A happy group from St Mary's RC Church prepare for a day trip aboard an Ogdens luxury coach in 1932.

Park Road Methodist Church, which was demolished and replaced by a modern building.

St Laurence's Church Lads' Brigade in 1930 on the Parish Church bowling green, Park Road. Leader Major Lofthouse is fourth from left, front row.

In July 1965, Chorley Parish Church celebrated 600 years of having a priest, although it is believed that a church has existed on the site since Saxon times.

Before Church Brow became steps. In Hollinshead Street on the right are the two houses which have become the Swann With Two Knecks. Below is Water Street, named to warn coach drivers of the need to cross the River Chor at the bottom of the hill. The tall building further back was the Parish Institute, long demolished.

Trinity Methodist Church will be 100 years old in 1995. Gillibrand Walks was the only road then. Most of the rest was fields and a footpath to the new Drill Hall.

Trinity Church Orchestra, well known in the locality. At the piano is Noel Sellars, a superb local organist. The occasion is probably the Sunday School anniversary with the assembled childrens', ladies' and gentlemen's choir.

St Mary's RC Church Centenary Committee in 1947. The picture was taken in St Mary's Old Church Hall. Clergy shown on right of the Mayor, Alderman Richard Evans, are Canon Cartmell, Fr Lydon and Fr Clayton.

Lessons Learnt

The Old Technical School, Chorley. The building is still used but is now the Town Library.

"Farewell Miss" – Mrs M.Salmon, assistant mistress at Weldbank St Gregory's RC School, receives a writing case from pupil Maureen Baxendale to mark her retirement after 40 years of teaching in the town. Left to right: Miss Calderbank, Mrs Kirkham, Mrs Salmon, Miss Grayken, Miss Lucas, Maureen Baxendale and headmaster Mr P.Turner.

Schoolchildren learn about the process of law and justice in proper surroundings. It will be noted from the furnishings, especially the dock with its spikes and bars, that this was the old Courtroom. While the new Courthouse was beng built, justice was dispensed in the Lancastrian Room of the Town Hall.

Class photograph of St Mary's RC Primary School 1956-57. The headmaster was Bernard Grime and teacher Mrs Fazackerley. The picture was taken outside St Mary's RC Church.

December 1960. More than 380 pupils moved from Chorley Grammar School to Parklands. However, as can be seen, the new school was not finished and 210 pupils had to stay in the old school while the new one was completed.

The original Chorley Grammar School at the turn of the century. The school, next to St Laurence's Church, was founded in 1611.

St George's Primary School is seen from Fleet Street in 1970. The house on the corner (left) was the Ring of Bells pub.

St George's Corner. St George's School was considered to have a most prominent site. There was talk of building Council Offices there if St George's moved – but the site was later used for the ill-fated Normid Superstore. St George's eventually moved to Carr Lane.

A concert party called
'The Somebody's' from
Water Street School,
around the time of World
War One.

Another concert party
group from Water Street
School at the same time.

Pupils of Duke Street School, 1930.

Class photograph taken in the playground of Hollinshead Street Infants' School in 1934.

National School class photograph from 1912. Miss Dicconson is the infant teacher. The school is thought to be that which was in Adlington.

National School class photograph of 1931– again, possibly Adlington.

Important Visitors

Coronation Street star Pat Phoenix, who played Elsie Tanner, hands over a cheque on behalf of the Inskip League to County Councillor Tom Jackson at a dance held at Leyland Motor's Club in the late 1960s.

Streetwise: Doreen Keogh and Ivan Beavis, stars of the early *Coronation Street*, kept young-sters happy for hours as they signed auto-graphs. The actors, who played Concepta and Harry Hewitt, appeared in town for a promotional visit in the early 1960s.

Prime Minister Harold MacMillan opens the Chorley stretch of the M6 in 1958.

Princess Margaret visited St Michael's School for its opening in October 1975. Excited pupils gathered in the hall, awaiting her arrival.

The Princess toured the school. Also seen here is the domestic science teacher, Miss Fisher.

Superintendent Joe Cook, president of Chorley and District Boys' Club, welcomes HRH the Duke of Gloucester (seated) who was to officially open the club in February 1957. The building was later destroyed by fire and replaced by a youth club.

A royal day for the Anderton Services on the M61. The Queen and Environment Secretary Peter Walker are seen leaving the opening of the services in October 1971.

When Willie Lowe was Mayor in 1946-47, he realised an ambition to make full use of the Town Hall Assembly Rooms. His charity ball was a big success, and the Assembly Hall was christened. The Lancastrian entertainer Tessie O'Shea played her part too, making sure the right tickets go to the right prizes.

Star visit: actors Fred Mawdesley, Norman Rossington, Michael Medwin and Charlie Drake visit the warping room of E.H.Cooper's Chorlex Mill in the late 1950s.

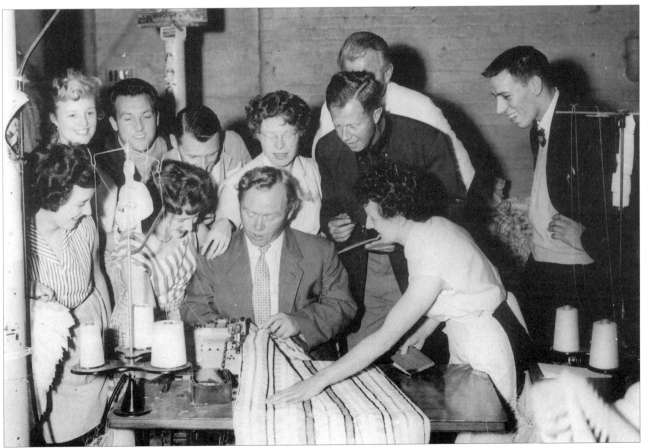

In stitches – Charlie Drake, seated, Michael Medwin, Norman Rossington and Fred Mawdesley with workers at the Chorlex Mill.

Celebrity visit – comedian
and actor Bob Monkhouse
with Lawrence Cooper,
right, at E.H.Cooper's
Chorley Mill weaving shed,
October 1957.

England and Preston
North End star Tom
Finney, third from left,
hands over prizes to
the winners of a cine-
camera competition at
the Odeon Cinema in
the 1950s.

Tom Finney opens the new extension of Coppull British Legion Club in the 1950s.

Chorley Societies

Girls from St Mary's choose the 1966 Hospital Queen at the first of the Chorley District Hospital Welfare Society's charity dances.

Members of Coppull St John's Church Mothers' Union with guests at their Christmas party held at the White Hart Hotel, Chorley, in the 1960s.

Members of Coppull St John's Church Lads' Brigade, inaugurated at the church in September 1965.

The Adlington Music and Arts Society members in their production of *Maritza* at the Christ Church School in 1965.

Scouts and Cubs from Leyland St Ambrose and Chorley ROF pack with their lanterns made from mangel-wurzels at a halloween gathering at Charnock Richard in November 1965.

Officials and guests at the Meat Traders' dinner, March 1955.

Chorley Amateur Dramatic Society performers in the panto, *Dick Whittington* in February 1955, at The Little Theatre, Dole Lane.

Guests and officials of Chorley Rotary Club President's Night in aid of charity on 13 March 1959.

The Heapey and Wheelton War Memorial Committee in August 1922, photographed in front of the clock tower, Wheelton. Sir John Jackson and Lady Jackson are in the centre of the first row.

Chorley Chamber of Commerce. It was a tradition to have a photograph taken and sent out as a Christmas card. The year is unknown.

Happy dancers at the Chorley Nonconformist Women's and Men's Bible Class old-time dance, held in the Town Hall in October 1951.

Coronation Celebrations

Proclamation of the Accession to the Throne on 21 June, 1901 of Edward VII (1901-1910).

Procession to celebrate the Coronation of King Edward VII in 1902. The Big Lamp was on the left, as is the Market Street Sunday School.

Another picture of the procession to mark the Coronation of King Edward VII in 1902.

Alderman W.Wilcock, father of the last mayor of the first Borough, was mayor at the proclamation in the Town Hall Square following the death of George V in 1936. The new King Edward VIII abdicated later in the year, to be succeeded by George VI.

A Coronation scene at Rice's Mill for King George VI in 1937.

Rice's weavers dressed up for the Coronation of George VI in 1937.

Swansey Mill at the time of the 1953 Coronation of Queen Elizabeth II.

This shop, on Market
Street, won prizes for
inside and outside dec-
oration to mark the
1953 Coronation.

Lawrence's Road Street
party for the Coronation
of Queen Elizabeth II in
1953.

In Carnival Mood

Children who took part in the fancy dress parade at St George's party, held in the vicarage grounds, July 1965.

The Mar-Jan Dancing School entered as the cast of *The King and I* in the 1965 Adlington Carnival.

Adlington St Paul's Youth Club members in their fancy dress display, 'Dr What' at the 1965 Adlington Carnival.

The *Chorley Guardian* float in the town carnival of 1958. Standing by the driver's cab is then editor, George Birtill.

Crowds at a Chorley Fairground, possibly pre-1910.

Children parade on horse-drawn waggons in what is thought to be the Rose Festival of 1925. The procession is seen in Bolton Road.

1924 Carnival Float called 'China Town'. It won first prize for being the most colourful float. This picture was taken at Whittle.

A carnival float called 'God's Helpers' from 1923. The photograph was taken in either Chorley or Whittle.

Chorley Walking Day

Chorley Walking Day in the early 1900s, on Park Road passing the Parish Institute.

A Chorley Walking Day before 1910.

Chorley Walking Day of 1911. The father of the girl in the black hat had died that Easter. St Laurence's group are seen here outside Booth's shop at the bottom of St George's Street. The children had red, white and blue flowers that year to mark the Coronation of George V.

Weldbank, walking past the old Town Hall (right) on Market Street. The photograph is rare – it is one of the few surviving which show the old Town Hall and the new Town Hall, on the left, in the same picture.

St Mary's RC parade on Walking Day, about 1920.

Walking Day, Park Road Methodist Church, date unknown.

Walking Day, Park Road Methodist Church, date unknown.

Chorley Walking Day in Market Street. The elderly gentleman with beard in the centre is William Hough, who had a baker's shop at 46 Pall Mall, Chorley.

Clifford Street, Chorley, passing Haydock's timber yard. St Laurence's Girl Guides on Walking Day, wearing navy blue dresses and orange ties.

The Boys' Brigade on Coronation Recreation Ground. Probably taken on Walking Day. This is where they would assemble before walking around the parish boundary. Date unknown, believed to be 1930s.

Chorley Walking Day, 1951. Irene and Lucille Love of St Laurence's Sunday School walking down Park Road.

July, 1965 – Small girls with baskets of carnations at Charnock Richard Walking Day.

1 July, 1965 – All Saints' Church Cub Scouts.

1 July, 1965 – St James's Church.

Sporting Chorley

A postcard showing the players of Chorley FC in the 1898-99 season.

Mighty Magpies – Chorley FC in 1957. Harry McShane, formerly of Manchester United, is pictured front right. His son, Ian, once a Chorley FC mascot, later went on to become an international film actor and star of TV's *Lovejoy*.

Adlington Hairpins football team in 1892.

Mining side: The Ellerbeck Dundee football team from the Ellerbeck coal mine, near Coppull, in 1908.

Adlington White Star football team. John Slater MP is third from the left on the back row. The photograph was taken on White Star Field on The Common in 1904.

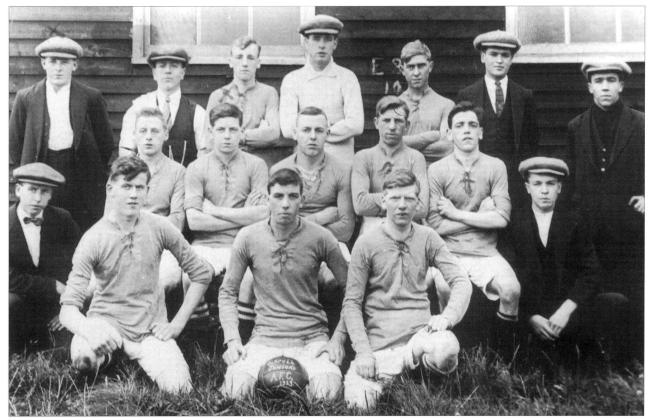

Coppull Juniors football team of 1923. Arthur Troughts is on the extreme right of the front row. He didn't live in Coppull, but most of his friends did. The young footballers won a gold medal each, but Troughts' father sold his when the family were hard-up.

Football team on St Laurence's Park, 1909. The land belonged to St Laurence's Park committee and was used as open space. The chimney in the background is a destructor chimney in Highfield Road.

Adlington St Paul's Men's Club football team in 1912.

Chorley Cricket Club team at Windsor Park, Chorley, 1910.

Chorley Cricket Club at Windsor Park, Chorley. Date unknown.

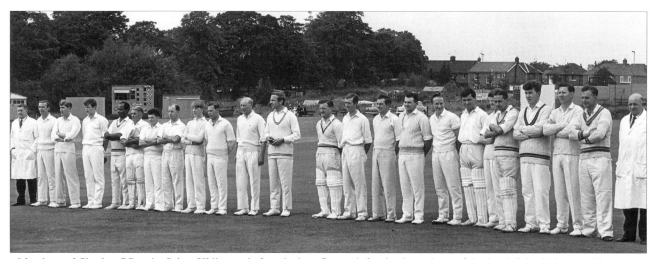

Members of Chorley CC and a Select XI line up before the benefit match for the dependents of the late Michael Norman. The game was played at Windsor Park on Sunday, 26 August 1965.

Adlington Cricket Club in 1904. Middle row, second from left, is Mr Middleton of Middleton's Mill.

Winners – Adlington Cricket Club won the Bolton and District Cricket Association Cup in 1914.

Adlington Cricket Club 1921, winners of the Gregg Cup, donated by Mr Gregg of Eagley Mill at Bolton.

Chorley Swimming Club about 1940. The building was in Railway Street and was privately owned.

September 1957 – St George's 'B' team, winners of the Chorley Churches Bowling League, receive their trophy from the Mayor of Chorley, Councillor T.Grime.

18 October 1957 – The annual prize distribution of the Northend Homing Society

Hut at Park Road tennis courts. On the right side was the ladies' changing room, on the left the men's changing room. In the middle was a refreshment bar. The picture was taken just after World War One.

A group of ladies on the tennis courts at Park Road in the 1920s. Anyone could play tennis there, although the courts were owned by Park Road Methodist Church.

Mr F.Phillips (centre) presents the Chorley and District Tennis League Shield to Windsor Tennis Club on 1 November 1957.

The hockey team at Chorley Grammar School, possibly 1934.

St Mary's RC Church Club, President's Day, 9 August 1958. Mr Francis Snape is being presented with the trophy.

Odds and Ends

Chorley Gas Works pictured in July 1956. Situated in Chorley Bottoms, this undertaking became famous. When a member of the council complained about a dreadful smell from Chorley Bottoms, he was referring to the undertaking which had belonged to the local authority from early days and was one reason why street lamps were lit by gas until after World War Two. Nationalisation removed this from Chorley's management, although two gasometers at the top of the hill are a landmark.

62 Lyon's Lane. Unremarkable by any standards, but this house was built in a day for a bet, although how long it actually took to construct is now the subject of debate.

The only remains of Duxbury Hall near what is now the municipally-owned Duxbury Park Golf Club.

The original newspaper shop at Higher Wheelton, situated on Blackburn Road. Standing in the doorway on the right is Mr Edward Tomlinson, the owner of the shop.

The Commercial Inn, Water Street, before the turn of the century.

Buckshaw Farm, Euxton, unseen by the public for many years because it lies in the middle of the restricted Royal Ordnance Factory grounds. This photograph was probably taken around 1910.

In September 1965, a weapons amnesty was declared. These were some of the frightening arms handed in at Chorley Police Station.

Hartwood was the estate of the Chorley family, who were regarded as Lords of the Manor by the Anglo-Saxon Chorleyites. Chorley Hall was used for the then Hartwood Hall by true Chorleyites.

The opening of Chorley Baths (now demolished) in 1938.

A wartime plane crash on the moors, which killed the pilot and five crew, is remembered above Lead Mine Valley. A memorial was
erected near the spot where many people observe Remembrance Day.

Arnold Wesker of Chorley, a great amateur entertainer, pianist and comedian. He performed lunch-time concerts during the war and once appeared on *Worker's Playtime*, a BBC radio programme. This photograph was taken when Wesker was a member of the Boys' Brigade. He was also a member of Park Road Methodist Church.

This picture was taken outside the Wheatsheaf in Coppull in 1914. The little boy in uniform at the front appears to be a mascot.

The Gillibrand Hall Gate, now a dignified entrance to Astley Park.

Astley Park Gate Gala. The picture shows the gate in its original situ at Gillibrand Hall. The decorated archway marks a wedding.

The original Astley Park Gates. This was the entrance to the park before it was given as a war memorial and the present gates from Gillibrand Hall were substituted.

Subscribers

Margaret Ainsworth

Margaret Akroyd

David & Rita Anderson

Paul D Archer

Tom Armstrong

Frank & Gladys Ashurst

Gladys Aspinall

Paul Atkinson

Thomas Atkinson

Mrs Elsie Audsley

Ivor Ayton

W Bailey

The Barker Family

Mr E G Barlow

Enid Beardsworth

John Beattie

Cllr & Mrs J E Bell

Mrs Boffey & Mr & Mrs Bennison

W T Berry

Dorothy Birchall

Mrs Edith Birchall

Tom Blythen

Patricia Nan Bolan

J Bolton

Jean Bond

David Leslie Bradley

Marjorie Bromley

Thomas Brooks

Mr F Brown

J A Brown

Don Brownley

Browns Butchers

Mabel Burgess

Mr & Mrs John Burke

Burns Jewellers Ltd

May Campbell

N K & C O Campbell

John & Pauline Carter

Henry Young Clarkson

Mr Brian Clayton

Agnes Clegg

Robert Cooper

Marilyn & Bob Crawford

Thomas Cuncannon

John Darbyshire

Mr J Denver

June Denver

Selina Denver

Mr John Devine

Mrs M E Dickinson

Mr P R Dickinson

Allen Douglas

Elizabeth C Douglas

John Eccles

Mr A Ellison

Mrs Patricia Ellison

Joan Ellithorn

Lily Fadden

Mrs Margaret Farnworth

Thomas Farnworth

Barbara M Fowles

Bernard Gallery

John Gill

Ruth M Gill

Thomas Clive Gillibrand

Sr Helen M Gormally

David Gough

Eleanor Graves

Frank Grayken

Mr Norman Greeney

Eric Greenhalgh

Gemma Gregory

Alice F Grieve

John D Grieve

Eric Allan Hall

Kevin Samuel Hall

Colin Harrison

Jimmy Harrison

Wilma Hartley

Elizabeth Heaton

Mr John William Heaton

Dorothy Hilton

Joe Holden

Sidney Holding

Donald A Holt

Jean Houghton

Maud Houghton

Mrs Winifred Howarth

D J & M Howlett

Catherine Hoyle

Maureen Hughes

Ethel Ikin

C Ingham

Catherine Ironfield

Alice Jackson

The Jackson Family

Mr Sidney Johnson

Brian Jolly

Ron Jolly

Ruth Jolly

Ellis Jones

Jean Jones

Michael Gerrard Keane

Mrs Denise Kelly

C Kerfoot

Mrs Jean King

Robert Knowles

Kathleen Langton

Sybil Langton

Frank & Audrey Latham

Barbara & Derek Latus

Michael T Lawson

Caroline Livesey

Frank Livesey

Ivy Lofthouse

Robin Logie

Brian Longton

Elsie Longton

The Love Family

Barry Lowe

Cllr J N Lucas JP

Patrick W V McLean

J T Makinson

Thomas H Marsland

Brenda Martland

Peter G Massey

David Mayock

Brian & Heather Milhench

Ronald & Ena Miller

Cllr Mrs F M Molyneaux

Sheila Ann Moon

K F Morris

Cyril J Moss

Colin Nightingale

Evelyn Norris

Patricia Oatley

Robert O'Malia

Andrew & Sharon Parkinson

George & Ann Parkinson

H Parkinson M.R.Pharm.S.

Pawsons Golden Plaice

Ruth Peach

Harry Pendlebury

Kevin Phillip

R Pilkington

Rosaleen Price

Billy Rainford

Mrs M Rainford

Mary Reeves

Audrey Reid

George Riding

Jean & Tony Rigby

Bette Rigg

K & B Riley

Mrs Doris Roberts

Mrs Mary Elizabeth Roberts (née Mary E Whittle)

Clive Robinson

Bill & Marie Roden

Dennis Rogers

K M Rogers

Mr & Mrs G Roscoe

P Roscoe

Rita Roscoe

Jennifer Rothwell

Cllr & Mrs Geoff Russell

Anne Schofield

John & Muriel Sharples

Ellen Sherratt

Counc. Mrs Edna Shone, JP

Alan G Smith

Evelyn Smith

John W Smith B.E.M.

Stapleton Fashions

Mrs Connie Stones

Ann Stringfellow

C E Stringfellow of Stringfellows, Chorley

Geoffrey Suter

George & Brenda Swann

Grace Swarbrick

Joseph Swarbrick

M Sweeney

Geoff & Doreen Taylor

J Taylor

J Taylor

Mr & Mrs S Taylor

Margaret Thorne

John Francis Townsend

Mrs D M Turner

Lena Vernon

Mrs Isobel Waldren

Florence Walmsley

Robert W Wareing

Joan Waring

Donald West

Keith West

Susan West

L Westhead

Susannah Wharton

Les & Jean Whitley

J H Whittaker

Bernie Whittle

Lilian Whittle

Gerald Wilcock

Mr Keith Wilding

Mrs Christine Williams

Annie Wilson

Brenda & Jim Winnard

Mary Winstanley (née Mary Parsons)

Sheila Wrennall

Eric Young

James Young